Pen It Forward

Pen It Forward

*Use Your Words to Spread Love
and Joy with a Handwritten Letter*

Ronna Vigil

The Heart to Heart Press

Littleton, Colorado

Pen It Forward: Use Your Words to Spread Love and Joy with a
Handwritten Letter
Published by The Heart to Heart Press™
Copyright © 2015 by Ronna Vigil. All rights reserved.

Library of Congress Control Number: 2015938650

SELF-HELP / Communication & Social Skills
SELF-HELP / Motivational & Inspirational

Vigil, Ronna
Pen It Forward: Use Your Words to Spread Love and Joy with a
Handwritten Letter

ISBN 978-0-9861083-0-3

This book is printed in the United States of America.

The Heart to Heart Press

I dedicate this book to
my precious mother,
my beloved husband,
and our glorious God

CONTENTS

INTRODUCTION

"Behind the dim unknown,
standeth God within the shadow,
keeping watch above his own."
- James Russell Lowell, 1844

"How sacred is the written word that paints portraits on our souls." -
Jennifer Martin, Chicken Soup for the Writer's Soul

I was wishing for a miraculous sign from God when I suddenly got one. Early one morning, I was talking to my friend on the phone wondering what I should do next with my life. What *was* I called to do?

Dawn startled me when she said, "It's finally time for you to write your book!" She said it with such conviction that it made me nervous. I knew she was right, though. We'd often talked about my dream of being a writer. I'd taken some writing courses and published a few articles, but I kept putting off writing a book.

I sighed. "I have no idea what to write about." Then we both rattled off some ideas, but none of them stuck or lit me up. "If God could just give me a sign," I sighed. "I wish He'd send me a fax with a clear answer."

At that very moment, I heard a beep on the line. It was "call waiting." On the other line was Kathryn Severns Avery, a new friend I'd met at a brainstorming gathering for women with heart-based business. We called it our "heart-storming" group. As soon as I ended the call with Dawn, I called her back ...

"I've been thinking about you and how you should write a book about the handwritten letter," Kathryn said. "People love receiving praise and appreciation. And getting

"Only passions, great passions, can elevate the soul to great things." - Diderot, 1746

a handwritten note is so rare these days. You could create a blueprint or guide."

I was stunned. I'd never told her about my secret desire to write a book, and yet she'd called me at the precise moment when I'd asked God for a clear sign—He never ceases to amaze me. I was overjoyed by the suggestion because I've had a passion for hand-writing notes and letters for many years. It's a beloved ritual I enjoy almost daily.

I first discovered this wonderful life- and love-enhancer when I read Alexandra Stoddard's *Gift of a Letter*.

When I began writing notes and letters, I had no idea how much it would enrich my relationships with others, but it quickly became clear. I soon noticed that the more I expressed appreciation to the people in my life, the happier they seemed and the more fulfilled I felt. My relationships became much richer. I've been truly touched by the positive response I've received from my family and friends.

I'll always remember when my mother told me, "Your gift is your words. You bless me with your words." Here I was wishing I could give her more financial support to make her life easier in her latter years, but it was my affectionate words and notes that meant the most to her.

"God enters by a private door into every individual."
- Ralph Waldo Emerson

For many years, my mother had been uncomfortable expressing praise and affection and voicing her feelings, so when she said this to me, it was immensely validating.

Writing to others has enriched my world, and I trust it will enrich yours as well. Please join me on a joyful journey of honoring and celebrating the precious people in our lives. I believe the world will be a better place, our homes a happier space and our relationships better than ever when we take time to show we care in notes and letters. Many of them will be treasured forever.

Thank you for opening this book and your heart. I wish you extraordinary love and happiness!

Ronna

1

COMPELLING REASONS TO WRITE A LETTER

"The beauty of being written to is the sense of importance it gives to us. It is immensely pleasing . . . to be singled out and acknowledged as someone worthy of a letter."
- Jennifer Williams, Victoria,
The Pleasures of Staying in Touch:
Writing Memorable Letters

"Only on paper has humanity achieved glory, beauty, truth, knowledge, virtue and abiding love." - George Bernard Shaw

What if you could freeze in time those precious moments of your life, those moments filled with gratitude, love, and joy? And what if you knew you could help fulfill one of the deepest needs of every human being? You can. You can do this with your pen.

I get so excited about all the wonderful reasons to write someone a note or a letter. We can:

- Express love and affection
- Convey gratitude and thankfulness
- Restore a relationship
- Spice up a stale romance
- Deepen intimacy
- Reciprocate a kindness
- Share warmth and friendliness
- Initiate a relationship
- Support and reassure
- Offer positive reinforcement
- Congratulate and celebrate
- Admire and pay a compliment
- Uplift and inspire
- Record a happy memory
- Create a keepsake of loving feelings and events.

"The supreme happiness of life is the conviction that we are loved."
- Victor Hugo

In the midst of writing this book and striving to capture the ultimate reason to sit down and write someone a letter, I was flipping through the television channels when something on OWN, the Oprah Network, caught my attention. A man was near tears and thanking Oprah for a valuable life lesson. While he was watching her show one day, she'd said, "The connection all of us share is a simple wish to be validated: 'Do you see me? Do you hear me? Does anything I say matter to you?' "In the midst of passionately pursuing his dream to be a famous singer, this man suddenly realized that what he really wanted was to feel validated.

It was a revelation for me, too! I'd found my answer: The fundamental reason we write a letter is to acknowledge and validate the recipient. We're letting them know that they matter, that their life makes a difference. To write a letter of praise and appreciation is to acknowledge people in a positive and powerful way. We're appreciating their existence. The written word is a wonderful way to value, affirm, and cherish someone.

What's more, when you write affirming notes or letters, you're making a positive difference not only to the recipients but to those around them as well. Joy is contagious. When

"What is hunger? It's a deep longing and a need to be truly known, accepted, respected, loved, valued, seen, and heard by the self and others." - Dr. Robin Smith

you make someone happy, I guarantee you they will make someone else happy, who will then make someone else happy, and the good feelings will go forth exponentially. What a satisfying feeling to know we've played a pivotal part. *We penned it forward!*

Besides being a significant way to make a contribution to another person, notes and letters can also help us feel connected. Abraham Maslow, an American psychologist best-known for "Maslow's hierarchy of needs," believed we could not experience true happiness or reach our full potential without first satisfying one of our most basic human needs; the need for connection. We require strong bonds of love and connection not only to thrive but to survive. Letters are a meaningful way to connect with a loved one. They can also reawaken and affirm feelings of love and belonging.

A few weeks ago I was feeling low, so I pulled out a box of letters and cards that I've been collecting for years. As I read through those treasures, I was overcome by the love and kindness expressed there. Cherished memories touched my heart, and my spirits were instantly lifted. Reading the notes and letters made me feel valued and cared for.

"Joy is contagious, commit to being a carrier."
- Kevin Harney, Seismic Shifts

There were cards and loving letters from my husband, my mother, my brother, my mother in-law and sister in-law, cherished friends, co-workers and neighbors. I have one box that is dedicated to Doreen, who has been a best friend and big sister to me. For more than twenty five years she has showered me with loving, supportive, life-giving words in gorgeous cards and lovely letters.

Rereading what they'd written warmed my heart. It was enormously validating. When I tucked the letters back into the box, I felt better. I had a special sense of belonging and connection.

I was especially excited to reread old love letters and notes from my husband. Without these written reminders, I may have forgotten what our love had been like in the beginning. It gave me goose bumps and butterflies to read and remember some of the exquisitely romantic things my sweetheart would say to me. He still does, but there's nothing like reliving the extraordinary feeling of falling in love with him. The treasured notes and letters he wrote made this possible.

I love acknowledging people in a note or letter because it allows me the freedom to express how I feel without embarrassment or distraction, which can easily set in during a conversation. Hand-writing letters helps me to be more openhearted. There's something sacred and special about sitting quietly with my pen and paper, something that opens a reservoir to my soul. It gives me a chance to slow down and reflect on my life and the love and appreciation I feel for others. I can devote my undivided attention and express my innermost feelings of affection. Pen and paper make it easier to say things I might hesitate to say out loud. Anne Morrow Lindbergh, author of, *Gift from the Sea,* says she meets people better in letters, and I feel the same way.

Of course, face-to-face conversations are essential to a fulfilling relationship, and in many cases these cherished encounters *are* the inspiration for my letters. I often get a burst of joy and excitement and, a deep sense of fulfillment from spending time with a loved one or a kindred spirit, especially when we've been engaged in a conversation that matters. I'm talking about those glorious moments when you move beyond the surface into a deeper, more meaningful discussion and you make a soul satisfying connection with another person.

Writing about our rich interactions with another can make a wonderful letter. I keep a pen and paper close by

"Love is not love until you give it away."
- Oscar Hammerstein

so I can write while the experience is still fresh and vivid in my mind.

Have you been inspired to write someone a note or a letter but didn't? What stopped you? Were you worried that you weren't a good enough writer? Perhaps you thought you didn't have the right words. Or maybe you felt apprehensive about exposing your feelings on paper. It could be that you considered it inconvenient or too much effort. Maybe something else came up and distracted you. Whatever the reason, it's possible you don't realize just how much the people in your life long for your recognition.

My husband affirmed this truth for me when he wrote: "Love, thank you for my love note. It was powerful & beautiful. I sure need and love your words."

A handwritten note or letter is a treasure because it's rare. Sending a text or an e-mail is easy and far too common, but sending a handwritten letter shows that we made a special effort. To me, it's pure pleasure to receive one. When I pick up my mail and see my name handwritten on a pretty envelope, it instantly gets my attention and elicits excitement.

In a culture immersed in technology, I was delighted to discover that I'm not the only one who feels this way. The

"When you write by hand you're more connected to your heart."
- Carrie Friedberg

---

other day I went to the store to stock-up on stationery, and right there in front of me were boxes of blank note cards that read, "Tired of Texting?" and "Going old school with a note-card."

I was thrilled that my passion for writing notes and letters isn't so old-fashioned after all. Perhaps those of us who realize that a handwritten letter is too valuable to ever go out of style are actually on the cutting edge.

Imagine writing a heart warming, soul-stirring letter that deeply touches someone forever. Picture someone special pressing your letter against his or her heart with a smile. This treasure from you can be tucked away and savored over and over.

2

HOW TO WRITE A LETTER

"This above all; to thine own self be true."
- William Shakespeare

"Will to be that self which one truly is."
- Soren Kierkegaard

The best way I can tell you to write a note or letter is simply to be yourself. Speak sincerely from your heart. Don't get caught up in trying to be clever or articulate, unless that's a natural part of your personality. If that's the case, then by all means do it! You can never go wrong by being yourself.

When I told my husband I was going to pick one of his letters to put in this book, he looked mortified. "You can't use my stuff!" he said. "I'm not a writer! You're the writer. What could you possibly pick that *I've* written?" Many people seem to feel this way about their writing, but writing a note or a letter doesn't require that you be a great writer. What makes a great letter is the heart and sentiment you put into it. My husband doesn't consider himself a writer and yet he's a soulful, passionate person and it shows in his writing. Some days his notes are simple and sweet or about some daily routine, and other days they make me weep.

So take comfort in the fact that our letters don't have to be polished and perfect, just sincere and heartfelt. Most of the time, I write straight from my heart and don't edit or make changes. I like the raw and spontaneous. After years

*"When you are content to be simply yourself and don't com-
pare or compete, everybody will respect you." - Lao-Tzu*

of practice, I can easily express what I want to convey most
days. The words come flowing out and are exactly what I
want to say. When I finish, I feel happy and satisfied.

But then there are those days when the words aren't
flowing and it's more of a challenge to express what I'm
feeling. I start … stop … can't seem to get going. It feels
choppy. I'm at a loss and wonder if I'll ever get it right.
Then I remember to get in touch with my heart and ask,
"What am I feeling for this person?" It's when I connect
with my heart that the words come to me.

I also like to pray. I request help from heaven. "Dear
God," I pray, "please guide me. What does my friend need
to hear today? What would You have me say? Thank You
for divine inspiration. Amen." Then I get quiet and listen.

I believe that if we ask, we will receive. As I receive, I jot
down the thoughts and keep writing. If something doesn't
come to mind right away, I wait a few minutes or until the
next morning. Inevitably fresh insights and inspiration
comes to me.

If we ask, we will receive.

3

THE BEST TIME TO WRITE
A NOTE OR A LETTER

"Do not keep the alabaster box of your love and friendship sealed up until your friends are dead. Fill their lives with sweetness. Speak approving, cheering words while their ears can hear them, and while their hearts can be thrilled and made happier. The kind things you mean to say when they are gone, say before they go."

- George W. Childs,

19th century American author

"You cannot do a kindness too soon because you never know how soon it will be too late." - Ralph Waldo Emerson

The time is now! Write while things are fresh in your mind and happily in your heart. Maybe you just shared quality time with someone special or had a meaningful conversation. Go grab your pen. Take notes. What did you love and appreciate about the conversation?

I write best when positive feelings are flowing. I love to capture the high of being with someone I care about on paper. Not only does it help me to remember special times together, but it also magnifies and multiplies the joy I feel. It makes the experience richer and more vivid. And I get to enjoy the experience all over again!

I always have writing supplies nearby—in my purse, in my car, all over the house. My collection includes pens, pencils and a variety of paper, cards, note cards, index cards, and favorite quotes. You never know when inspiration will strike. Tender feelings may wash over us when we're taking a bath, walking the dog, lounging in the sun or saying a prayer.

Be sure to give yourself plenty of time during the day to pause and be peaceful. This may seem odd to mention or irrelevant to letter-writing, but it's essential. If we're continually rushing from one event to the next, we risk

"Learn to pause or nothing worthwhile will catch up to you."
- Ancient Proverb

missing the moments in life that make it meaningful and worthwhile. If we don't slow down, we can miss those lovely little miracles that are potentially everywhere. We must take time to rest and be quiet. Find a way to have uninterrupted time to reflect and savor what's truly important, even if it's only five minutes.

Last week it dawned on me that I hadn't written a single note or letter. That's unusual for me, and I wondered how this had happened. Then I realized it was because I was overly tired. I was going to bed later than usual and not getting up early enough to practice my beloved ritual.

Over the years, I've learned that if I don't take time to nurture myself, the quality of attention I give to others suffers. My enthusiasm and zeal for people fades when I feel out of balance. I'm better able to express love and appreciation when I'm well-rested. Patricia Spadaro addresses this marvel in *Honor Yourself: The Inner Art of Giving and Receiving* as do Cheryl Richardson in *The Art of Extreme Self Care* and Lucille Zimmerman in *Renewed: Finding Your Inner Happy in an Overwhelmed World*, three of my favorite books on the subject.

Taking time to slow down and care for ourselves isn't a luxury, it's a vital necessity. Trust me, it's not selfish—it's self-preservation—and *everyone* benefits.

"I loaf and invite my soul."
- Walt Whitman

PROMPTS

Start a journal. As part of my letter-writing ritual, I warm up by journaling on a legal-size pad of paper in a variety of colors. I try to write something every morning. I love this practice. Julia Cameron calls it "Morning Pages." It warms me up for all kinds of writing. Some days I write at the top of my paper, "Today's Heart's Desires," and make a wish list for my day of how I want it to unfold. It includes things I would love to see happen for me and for my friends and family. This also gets me thinking about the people in my life.

The most important thing to keep in mind is, the more you write for your-self, the more comfortable you'll be writing to someone else. The more you put your pen to paper, the easier it will become. Journaling

"He makes me lie down in green pastures, he leads me beside peaceful waters, he restores my soul." - Psalm 23:2-3

is also therapeutic and can bring clarity to your life and your hopes and dreams.

I'm a morning person, so I'm at my best when I rise early. My energy is high and cheerful, and that's the ideal time for me to reach out to people. With a pretty round stationery box labeled "Love" next to me, I sit on our comfy love seat with a hot cup of tea and write away.

If you're a night owl and enjoy the hush of evening, take advantage of this quiet time when everyone else is sleeping. Create a ritual that works well for you, but be open to spontaneity, too. Although I write most of my letters in the morning, I make notes about the people I appreciate throughout the day.

Whatever works best for you, don't put it off until tomorrow. Chances are someone you love and care about needs to hear from you today.

4

THE BEAUTY OF
APPRECIATION

*"If you treat a man as he is, he'll stay
as he is, but if you treat him as if he were
what he ought to be, and could be, he will
become the bigger and better man."*
- Johann Wolfgang von Goethe

"The way to develop the best that is in a man is by appreciation and encouragement." - Charles Schwab

---

Our words can help feed the deepest need of another human being, the need to know he matters, the need to know we care. People crave this acknowledgment almost as much as we need air.

William James, the father of American psychology, said, "The deepest principle in human nature is the craving to be appreciated." To appreciate means to give thanks, and it also means to value, treasure, and hold in high regard. To appreciate is to recognize, validate, and affirm.

We can give a meaningful gift to others by acknowledging the good in them. A wonderful way to do this is with a pen.

For my brother-in-law's fiftieth birthday, I thought our family members could honor him by listing fifty things we respect, admire, and appreciate about him. All eight of us were more than happy to write lists of six things we love about Orley, and Orley's wife, Michelle, happily volunteered to write the extra two.

At the dinner celebration, which happened to be on Thanksgiving Day, we each read our list to him and then gave him our lists as mementos. The outcome was even better than I'd expected. Orley sat quietly and humbly took in everything we read, and then he surprised us by

"Compliments are like glue that holds a relationship together."
- Unknown

going around the room and graciously expressing what he appreciated about each one of us. A heart-touching mix of laughter and tears, it was a beautiful experience. It still gives me goose bumps just thinking about it.

Compliments, sincerely given, can go beyond the present moment and make a lifelong impact. Yet, all too often we stop short of writing kind words to others because we're busy or, embarrassed or think that what we have to say won't mean much to the other person. But there are few things on earth as priceless and affirming as sincere praise and acknowledgment.

I once read a story about a Franciscan nun whose classroom assignment became a treasure for many of her students. But she didn't know this until she attended the funeral of Mark Eukland, a young man who was killed in the line of duty in Vietnam. Mark had been in one of her elementary school classes and years later in a junior high class, so she had a chance to get to know him a little better than many of her students, and he was always a favorite. When she arrived at the funeral, Mark's father said, "We want to show you something," and handed her two worn pieces of notebook paper that had obviously

"The roots of all goodness lie in the soil of appreciation for goodness." - Dalai Lama

---

been taped, folded, and refolded many times. "They found these on Mark when he was killed. We thought you might recognize it."

Sister Helen said she knew without looking that the notebook paper contained the kind words of all of Mark's junior high classmates. The pages were from an assignment she'd given to the students to improve their mood and lift their spirits. "Write out the nicest thing you can think of about each of your classmates," she'd instructed. After collecting the papers, she made a list for each student of all the kind words the other students wrote about him or her. Within minutes of receiving them, all her students were smiling and she heard them whispering things like, "Really? I never knew that meant anything to anyone."

At the funeral home, Mark's mother expressed her great gratitude. "As you can see, Mark treasured it."

"That's when I sat down and cried," Sister Helen said. "I cried for Mark and for all his friends who would never see him again. The density of people in society is so thick that we forget that life will end one day, and we don't know when that one day will be. So please, tell the people you love and care for that they are special and important. Tell them before it's too late."

"Everybody likes a compliment."
- Abraham Lincoln

That's the purpose of this book—to stir your heart to action and urge you to acknowledge those you hold dear. Life is fragile and fleeting -make it matter. Make it sweet. Let's seize every opportunity to cherish our friends and family. Now. Today. We can't assume that they can read our minds or know what sits quietly in the center of our heart. They won't know unless we tell them. Don't wait. Do it now, in a note or a letter.

PROMPTS

Who can you think of who would benefit from a kind word or a compliment? Your teacher, a mentor, a friend's mother or father? It could be anyone you appreciate, admire, or adore. Keep in mind that, no matter how successful or confident people appear, they need a reassuring word as well. Your boss, a co-worker, or a friend from school, longs for appreciation and approval as much as you do. So do your husband, your sister, your parents and your grown

"I can live for two months on a good compliment."
- Mark Twain

---

child. Most people are hungry, if not starved for positive reinforcement and enthusiastic recognition. We can never hear too many times that we're valuable, wonderful, and worthwhile.

Warm up with this:
- ♥ You are important to me because…
- ♥ The great thing about you …
- ♥ What I admire, appreciate, or adore about you …
- ♥ I'll always remember when …
- ♥ It means so much to me when you …
- ♥ You make me feel …
- ♥ My favorite thing about being with you …

Say the nicest things you can think of. "Even if your plaudits run a little ahead of reality," says Fred Bauer, author of *The Power of a Note*, "remember that expectations are often the parents of dreams

"It is only with the heart that one can see rightly; what is essential is invisible to the eye." - Antoine De Saint-Exupery

fulfilled." Be sincere and be generous. Cast people in the most favorable light possible. Don't hesitate to lavish them with terms of praise like *"remarkable," "talented,"* and *"incredible."* Include specific examples of what makes them so. Write down everything you love and appreciate about them. Think of things they've said or done that you're especially grateful for. Point out their good qualities. Notice their strengths. You could even include positive things you've heard other people say about them. Add every little thing you can think of.

It's an eye-opening and enriching experience to capture what we love and enjoy about others on paper. As we reflect and write, the list tends to grow longer and our appreciation and affection for them can grow stronger. Start small if you're uncomfortable with praising people, but be sure to do it. Then revel in the pleasure you get.

And you just might find that others are more inclined to lavish you with more praise and appreciation too.

5

THE GIFT OF GRATITUDE

"If you concentrate on finding what is good in every situation, you will discover that your life will suddenly be filled with gratitude, a feeling that nurtures the soul."
- *Rabbi Harold Kushner*

"The miracle of gratitude works inside and out, backward and forwards." - Penelope Stokes

One morning as I pulled out of the garage, our neighbor Svetlana came rushing toward me with a sweet twinkle in her eye. I rolled down the window and she grabbed my face and kissed me.

"Your words," she said in her endearing Russian accent, "I never received such words."

I had written Svetlana and her husband, a retired couple we've lived next door to for sixteen years, a "thank-you" note telling them how much we appreciated their arranging a four day stay for us at their time-share condo in the Colorado resort town of Steamboat Springs. I wanted to acknowledge them for this kind act as well as for being so consistently generous to my husband and I over the years.

Svetlana wanted to be sure I knew how much my words of gratitude meant to her, and seeing her so happy made my *own* heart sing. Who doesn't light up when someone sincerely values something we've said or done? I certainly relish the recognition I receive. And it makes us want to do even more for those grateful souls. It's beautiful how reciprocal thankfulness can be.

Gratitude is good for both the giver and receiver. Steve Toepfer, assistant professor of human development

"Silent gratitude isn't very much to anyone."
- Gertrude Stein

and family studies at Kent State University, has done research that confirms it. He conducted a study involving more than two hundred men and women to assess how writing "thank-you" letters affected them. It makes sense that words of gratitude make the receiver feel great, but he wondered what the benefits to the writer are.

The people in Toepfer's study were instructed to write three meaningful letters of gratitude over three weeks, spending ten to fifteen minutes on each. Not just a simple "thank you" but sincere, heartfelt expressions of appreciation. The results? He discovered that the more the subjects wrote, the better they felt. In fact, the majority of people who wrote letters of appreciation reported feeling happier and more satisfied with their lives overall. They even had fewer symptoms of depression.

You can even go a step further than letter-writing and make a "gratitude visit." Martin Seligman, Ph.D., former president of the American Psychology Association and a leading expert in gratitude therapy, did a study in which participants randomly received one of six therapeutic interventions to improve their quality of life. The intervention that proved to be most effective was the "gratitude visit," in which the participant wrote a letter of

> *"No duty is more urgent than that of returning thanks."*
> *- James Allen*

---

appreciation and delivered it. This simple act caused the participant's happiness scores to rise significantly. Even more, the "gratitude visit" had a positive impact on the letter writer for as long as a month afterward.

Not only will you enhance your happiness and well-being through writing notes and letters of gratitude, but you'll also significantly enhance the quality of your relationships.

Reassuring words can strengthen our bonds with each other and bring us great pleasure and deep satisfaction, especially if being appreciated is what makes us feel most loved and valued.

In *The 5 Love Languages: The Secret to Love That Lasts,* a *New York Times* best-seller for over twenty years, Dr. Gary Chapman lists words of affirmation as one of the five primary love languages. If it happens to be your mate's main love language, expressing words of gratitude and appreciation can be absolutely essential to the success of your relationship.

Dr. Chapman assures us that if we learn and consistently practice expressing our mates' main love languages, we will enjoy an exciting and lasting love-affair that goes beyond

"We can only be said to be alive in those moments when our hearts are conscious of our treasures." - Thornton Wilder

anything we've ever dreamed of. But no matter what our primary love language is, we all want to know we are appreciated.

One morning while I was working on this book, a tidal wave of joy and gratitude washed over me. Here I was happily at home working on my book project and feeling full of passion, peace, and purpose. And I couldn't help but feel grateful for my husband. Without his spirited support, financial and emotional, I may not have pursued my deep desire to be a writer. Ever. So I grabbed my pen and a sheet of paper and wrote him a letter thanking him for helping me make my heart's desire possible. I acknowledged every sacrifice he'd made to help me, and every sweet and supportive word. I wanted him to know how truly thankful I was for who he is and what he's done.

I'll never forget the sound of his voice on the phone that night, the deep satisfaction in his tone as he told me how much my letter meant to him.

Read, study, pray about and practice gratitude and thankfulness every day, and resolve to be a regular, "thank-you card" giver. Gratitude is essential to the health of our relationships (and the people in them.) It's vitally important to acknowledge and thank people who give us a gift, do

"Feeling gratitude and not expressing it is like wrapping a present and not giving it." - William A Ward

something special or helpful and go out of their way for us. Never take a kindness for granted. We can't assume people know we're grateful—we need to tell them. Sure, we can say, "thank you" and go on our way, but taking time to write a note or a card is so much more meaningful. We don't know the last time someone received words of appreciation, and a card gives them something to savor and hang on to.

Be sure to thank people who may easily be over-looked, the people who serve and support us in a variety of ways. Even though we may pay them for a service, they deserve and desire recognition and appreciation and can too often be taken for granted: a favorite doctor, our beloved pet's vet, a helpful neighbor, the computer programmer who rescued our files, the book-keeper or accountant who saved us money, the handy-man who fixed something, the sweet lady at your child's day care, the plumber, the baby-sitter—you get the picture. Notice everyone around you and go out of your way to send a "thank-you" note.

I've often wished I could send a great big, "Thank You!" to God. But there isn't a card or sheet of paper big enough to contain the gratitude I feel for my life and those in it. So I write to God in my gratitude journal and hope the loving Creator is looking over my shoulder.

"He is a wise man who does not grieve for the things which he has not, but rejoices for those which he has." - Epictetus

PROMPTS

Get a journal or a legal pad and write: "Thank You, God for ..." or write "My Book of Blessings," or "My Gratitude List" or "Things And People I Feel Thankful For." Title it whatever you wish but be sure to include all the kind and helpful things people say and do.

But don't just think about it. Do it! Recording your blessings on paper is powerful. As you make a faithful practice of listing the good in your life (and there is *always* something to be thankful for), you will draw more good to you. A grateful person is rewarded often. Plus, you'll enjoy a more positive perspective on life and it will influence those around you. The world needs your joy and enthusiasm.

As for those days when you aren't feeling grateful or cheerful, you can look

"God gave you a gift of 86,400 seconds today. Have you used one to say 'thank you'?" - William A. Ward

at your list and get an instant lift, a lovely reminder of the blessings that fill your life. If they aren't written down, we can easily forget. When your list is done, you can use it as a springboard for writing "thank-you" notes and letters.

On Thanksgiving Day, for example, you might write down everything you feel thankful for and read it at the dinner table. Being around grateful people feels good and you can lift the mood of everyone in the room. Encourage your family to participate as well.

6

THE PEARL OF ENCOURAGEMENT

"At times our own light goes out and is rekindled by a spark from another person."

- Albert Schweitzer

"No one is useless in this world who lightens the burden of another."
- Charles Dickens

Marilyn Monroe was one of the most beloved movie actresses in history, with adoring fans across the globe. Yet she was frequently immobilized by insecurity and fear. She suffered from self-doubt and questioned her worth—something we all experience from time to time.

We all have some area of life where we lack confidence and courage. Daily challenges, set backs, and negative messages can weigh us down, and it's tempting to think we can't keep up or we aren't good enough. How refreshing when others give us positive reinforcement and remind us that we're worthwhile and special just as we are.

Marilyn had an acting coach, Paula Strasberg, who did more than teach technique. She was a trusted friend who played a pivotal part in building Marilyn up. She was a constant source of encouragement, filling Marilyn's ears with positive reassurance. As a reminder of Paula's love and support, Marilyn kept a handwritten note in which Paula had drawn a heart and written just two words, "Have faith."

Often, others can see our goodness and potential more clearly than we can. We all need someone who will cheer us on, someone who sees and believes the best in us. The world needs more people who are willing to call forth the promise in others. Just one encouraging word can be

"A word of encouragement does good."
- Proverbs 12:25

the spark needed to help us achieve something we never dreamed possible.

I am so thankful to have friends who believe in me and encourage me. When I was in the beginning stages of writing this book and gathering ideas and putting the pieces together, I became seriously discouraged and questioned my ability to make it happen. Just as I was tempted to give up and call it quits, my friend Dawn asked to see a copy of what I had so far. She lives forty minutes away and it was eight o'clock at night, so I e-mailed her my rough draft.

Two hours later she responded with such excitement and enthusiasm that I couldn't help but feel encouraged and eager to begin again. Her words breathed new life into me. Although her praise and reassurance came through an e-mail and not the postal service, they were invaluable. I felt renewed and passionate once again about my project. It was immensely helpful to print what she wrote and read it over and over again. Not only that, but I was thrilled to learn that the very next morning Dawn went shopping for stationary and wrote a special letter to each of her children. I received a wonderful handwritten letter as well.

My friend had given me confirmation that what I was doing was worthwhile. Her zealous words reinvigorated me and kept me moving forward.

"Our words have the power to push people to their divine destiny and full potential." - Joel Osteen

Howard Schultz, the chairman and CEO who transformed Starbucks, said, "I really genuinely believe that if you tell people that they have what it takes to succeed, they'll prove you right."

Many successful people have become successful because they had someone who believed in them and took the time to say so, such as a loving grandmother, a coach, a special teacher, or a supportive spouse.

In *A Hand to Guide Me,* Academy Award Winner Denzel Washington shares inspiring stories from leading personalities in sports, politics, business, and the arts about the people who shaped their lives for the better.

Denzel also reveals his own story about growing up in Mount Vernon, New York, where he was blessed to have a handful of people who influenced his life and decisions in positive ways. One powerful presence was his English teacher at Fordham University, Robinson Stone. Stone was also an actor and involved in the theater program. When Denzel was auditioning for graduate-school programs in drama, Stone gave him the positive push he needed in the form of a recommendation letter. Denzel carries the letter to this day.

"The best way to find yourself is to lose yourself in the service of others." - Mahatma Gandhi

"Bob Stone's words—back then, they kept me going … He gave me something to live up to. He lit a fire in me … This man believed in me, and that was huge … And because he believed in me, I believed in myself."

Belief in someone can be expressed in many ways. To encourage means to inspire with courage, confidence, and spirit. It also means to provide support and hope. We can encourage someone who has endured heartache and loss, and we can give hope to someone who's discouraged, hopeless or stuck. Maybe we can remind someone who has forgotten or never realized what a gift her presence on earth is. I love the ancient story of the cracked pot:

An elderly Chinese woman had two large pots, each hung on the ends of a pole that she carried across her neck. One of the pots had a crack in it, while the other pot was perfect and always delivered a full portion of water. At the end of the long walks from the stream to the house, the cracked pot arrived only half-full.

For a full two years this went on daily, with the woman bringing home only one and a half pots of water. Of course, the perfect pot was proud of its accomplishments, but the poor cracked pot was ashamed of its imperfection and

"The heart sees better than the eye."
- Jewish Proverb

_____

miserable that it could do only half of what it had been made to do.

After two years of what it perceived to be bitter failure, it spoke to the woman one day by the stream. "I am ashamed of myself because this crack in my side causes water to leak out all the way back to your house."

The old woman smiled, "Did you notice that there are flowers on your side of the path, but not on the side of the other pot? Because I have always known about your flaw, I planted flower seeds on your side of the path, and every day while we walk back you water them. For two years I have been able to pick these beautiful flowers to decorate the table. Without you being just the way you are, there would not be this beauty to grace the house."

— as told by Arielle Ford, author of *Wabi Sabi Love*.

What a glorious gift to have someone willing and eager to look beyond our perceived limitations and flaws and see our unique contribution. We can give that gift to others. Be committed to bringing out the best in others—there are already enough fault-finders. Choose to be a blessing-giver.

"Encourage each other daily."
- Hebrews 3:13

PROMPTS

Can you think of someone in need of encouragement? Look both within and beyond your immediate circle. Be generous, open-minded and big-hearted. Extend your list to include your neighbor, someone at church, a person from school or at work. Maybe it's the boy or girl next door who's shy and awkward and in deep need of approval. Your note could inspire a new glow of confidence in that child. Rest assured that your written words carry energy and power.

Go grab a pen and paper. Encourage someone today in a note or a letter.

7

THE MARVEL OF
A MINI-LETTER

*"If you want happiness for an hour, take
a nap. If you want happiness for a day,
go fishing. If you want happiness for a year,
inherit a fortune. If you want happiness
for a lifetime, help somebody."*
- Chinese Proverb

"There is no exercise better for the heart than reaching down and lifting people up." - John Holmes

We don't need to write a long letter to make a lasting impact. A few crucial words can make a big difference. On my thirtieth birthday, my friend's older sister sent me a lovely little book called, *"She Who Loves a Garden,"* by Mary Engelbreit. Inside she inscribed only two short lines: "To Ronna, One of God's beautiful creations on her 30th Birthday. We love you." Just two lines, yet they made such an impression on me. I didn't see myself as a beautiful creation. At that time, I was single and living alone. I felt unlovable and disconnected. But Debbie's caring gesture affirmed and comforted me. The gift was totally unexpected, and I was touched that she saw me as special. She was my friend's sister and I didn't know she'd really noticed me. And the message of the book she'd chosen mirrored her handwritten note. "She who loves a garden likes to make the earth more lovely and enjoys the beauty she's contributing," One page read. Debbie seemed to be acknowledging the good in me and saying my presence made a difference.

Eighteen years later, I still cherish her gift. That short inscription was priceless to me. What if Debbie had called me instead of writing that sweet little message? I may not have remembered the call or been so touched. But she took the time to sow a positive seed, and it blossomed in me.

> *"Set a high value on spontaneous kindness."*
> *- Samuel Johnson*

It's amazing what a few affirming words can do to boost someone's morale and self-esteem.

The Note

In his article, "The Power of a Note," published in *Reader's Digest* in 1991, inspirational writer Fred Bauer recalled receiving a note at the age of fifteen while working at his first job, as sports editor for the Montpelier, (Ohio,) *Leader Enterprise.* "The envelope bore the logo of the closest big-city paper, *The Toledo Blade*," he said. "When I opened it, I read: 'Sweet piece of writing on the Tigers. Keep up the good work.' It was signed by Don Wolfe, the sports editor … His words couldn't have been more exhilarating." Fred kept that note in his desk drawer until it became "rag-eared." Whenever he doubted his ability to be a writer, he would reread the note and "walk on air." Ultimately, he became a well-known writer who brought hope and inspiration to thousands.

What if Don Wolfe had withheld that compliment? What if he'd been too busy or felt as if he were above such gestures? Had Fred not received those encouraging words, he might not have gone on to write *Norman Rockwell's*

> *"Good words are worth much and cost little."*
> *- George Herbert*

Faith of America and *Billy Graham: Personal Thoughts on a Public Man.*

Sending a handwritten note is significant because it gives the recipient something tangible to hold on to and look at. Fred reread that note countless times for reassurance, and that inspired him to keep writing.

The Postcard

I met Owen at a conference in Colorado. Making small talk, he casually asked me what I was up to. I enthusiastically told him about my book project, thinking I'd have to convince him that writing notes and letters was important. He surprised me.

"Have I got a story for you," he said. "In 2004, the CEO of our company was sick in the hospital. I sent him a postcard with a basset hound looking worn-out and tired. The dog was lying on some old tires at a junk yard. I sent Carl this postcard with a note that wished him well. Would you believe several years later I learned he still carries that post card? He showed it to me."

It had taken Owen less than five minutes to send that post-card, but Carl treasured it half a decade later.

Owen is an instructor for the Job Corps. In addition

"I believe . . . that every human mind feels pleasure in doing good to another." - Thomas Jefferson

to helping prepare his students for successful careers, he gives them advice on life issues such as the importance of appreciating our parents. He urges students to acknowledge and connect with their parents through post cards. "Most of the younger generation likes to send a text, but it's not the same," he said. "I tell them, 'Your mother wants to look at that postcard and notice your writing, maybe the special way you make your G's.' She'll hold it close to her chest and even smell the paper for a familiar scent of you. You can't get that from a text."

The Post-it Note

It works both ways—there's also nothing like getting a loving hand-written note from a parent. After all these years, seeing my mother's handwriting comforts me, especially when she calls me, "Ronna Lee." I'm transported to my childhood, when my mother's love was everything.

A few days after Mom stayed at our house to care for our dog while we were on vacation, I discovered a little note from her. She'd written on a pretty pink Post-it-Note and signed it, "XOXOXOXOXO Love you, Mom." I keep it where she left it in my desk drawer. It warms my heart every time I see it.

"A generous action is its own reward."
- William Walsh

Daily Love Notes

My husband and I have a note-writing ritual, a habit we got into about ten years ago. Before I leave for work every day, I write something to my hubby on a pad of paper and leave it for him on the kitchen counter. Some days my note is short and sweet. Other days I make a long list of things I love and appreciate about him; I love to acknowledge what a good man he is and all the good he does for me. I was touched to learn that the first thing he does when he comes home for lunch is head for my love note. And I do the same—when I get home, I rush to the kitchen to read what he's written.

"I love our notes to each other," he told me. "I like that it keeps us connected when we're apart." Daily love notes can keep couples closely connected. Writing to each other on a regular basis can be a loving, affectionate practice that fosters intimacy, good will, and happiness.

"If we give love its proper expression, our life unfolds like a beautiful flower." - William Fischer

PROMPTS

Start a daily love-note ritual. Write words of appreciation or a flirty comment. Say something to keep you connected. Be spontaneous and create an element of mystery. Put the notes in fun or unexpected places. Surprise him by putting one in his lunch box or gym bag, on his dashboard, in his shirt pocket or suitcase, on his pillow, at his workplace, or in a locker at his health club. Mail one to him or go all out and do a treasure hunt. Write little notes that lead to other notes that eventually lead to a climactic surprise.

You can also create a collage of little love notes written on pretty pieces of paper or mini-cards and put them in a nice notebook or a journal and give it to him.

"You know you're in love when you can't fall asleep because your reality is finally better than your dreams." - Dr. Seuss

Begin a note with:
- ❦ You make me feel …
- ❦ You are so … to me
- ❦ The great thing about you …
- ❦ What I love and adore about you …

You can also send postcards. Collect them when you travel, or get some from your local museum or gift shop.

The next time you buy a book for a family member or friend, inscribe a loving message.

8

THE BLESSEDNESS
OF LOVE

"There is no difficulty that enough love will not conquer: no disease that love will not heal: no door that enough love will not open ... It makes no difference how deep set the trouble: how hopeless the outlook: how muddled the tangle: how great the mistake. A sufficient realization of love will dissolve it all. If only you could love enough you would be the happiest and most powerful being in the world."

- Emmet Fox

"A flower cannot blossom without sunshine, and a man cannot live without love." - Max Muller

W hat if you didn't have to search for meaning in your life? What if you knew with every fiber of your being that the purpose of your life is to love?" asks Joan Borysenko, Harvard-trained medical scientist and best-selling author.

Love gives our life meaning. It makes life worth living. In *Man's Search for Meaning*, widely considered to be one of the most influential books in America, Viktor E. Frankl, a neurologist and psychiatrist who survived the Holocaust, tenderly conveys that love is the highest goal to which human beings can aspire. After his experience in the Auschwitz concentration camp, he wrote, "For the first time in my life, … I grasped the meaning of the greatest secret that human poetry and thought had to impart: the salvation of man is through love and in love."

It's true. We were created for love. And everyone who has tasted the sweetness of love, if even for a fleeting moment, can attest to its power. There are more famous quotes, stories, letters, movies, songs and scriptures about love than about any other subject. Love fortifies our whole being.

As a beautiful bonus, love and intimacy promotes vibrant health and well-being, physically and emotionally.

"I like not only to be loved, but also to be told I am loved."
- George Eliot

Dr. Dean Ornish, a cardiologist and *New York Times* best-selling author of *Love & Survival: 8 Pathways to Intimacy and Health*, says, "When you feel loved, nurtured, cared for, supported, and intimate, you are much more likely to be happier and healthier. You have a much lower risk of getting sick and, if you do, a much greater chance of surviving ... I am not aware of any other factor in medicine that has a greater impact on our survival than the healing power of love and intimacy. Not diet, not smoking, not exercise, not stress, not genetics, not drugs, not surgery."

So how can we foster more love and intimacy in our lives? By being willing to live and love with our whole heart and by being open to and generous with our love and affection. But that's not easy. It requires that we allow ourselves to be vulnerable. Brene Brown, Ph.D., best-selling author of *Daring Greatly*, has spent over a decade studying vulnerability and human connection. "Embracing our vulnerabilities is risky but not nearly as dangerous as giving up on love, belonging and joy," she says.

We're wired for connection and love, and there are many ways we can create meaningful connections and expressions of love. One of the most romantic and timelessly treasured is through a handwritten letter.

"We loved with a love that was more than love."
- Edgar Allan Poe

A love letter can:

- ❤ Deepen your connection and improve communication
- ❤ Strengthen your relationship and create a solid, sacred union
- ❤ Promote harmony and happiness in your relationship
- ❤ Express appreciation and validation to your mate
- ❤ Reveal or affirm feelings of love and affection
- ❤ Spice up your love life and rekindle a romantic flame
- ❤ Restore a wilting relationship
- ❤ Fuel fun, passion, and pleasure
- ❤ Ignite excitement and surprise

A love letter can also be a wonderful reminder of the presence of love when we need it most. Not long ago, one of my friends was feeling frustrated with her husband. She was lonesome and felt neglected. Her husband is a wonderful man, but he'd been working long hours and not physically or emotionally available to her as much as she'd have liked. One day while she was cleaning out a drawer, she found a card he'd given her, and her heart instantly softened. Seeing his hand-written note of love and affection

"One word frees us of all the weight and pain of life:
That word is love." - Sophocles

gave her a reassuring reminder of just how much he loves her.

This made all the difference in her attitude. A positive shift was initiated because she had a sweet memento of his love, an assuring word in a handwritten note to her, something she could hold on to and read over and over. That's the gift of a letter. He could have sent a lavish display of the most beautiful bouquet, but a love letter will live forever.

Recently while reading *I Love You, Ronnie: The Letters of Ronald Reagan to Nancy Reagan,* I wondered if President Reagan and the first lady's passionate marital love-affair of nearly fifty years would have been different had he not expressed his love, thoughts, and feelings for her in his handwritten letters. President Reagan wrote to his beloved from California's governor's office, from Air Force One, from filming locations during his acting career, and even while sitting in the same room with her. On their thirty-first anniversary, he wrote, "I more than love you. I am not whole without you. You are life itself to me. When you are gone, I'm waiting for you to return so I can start living again."

Strong evidence that love letters can create a powerful connection between two people.

"Out of your vulnerabilities will come your strength."
- Sigmund Freud

PROMPTS

Write a love letter to your mate. Let "How Do I Love Thee?" (Sonnet 43), by Elizabeth Barrett Browning, inspire you to list what you love about your sweetheart. Mention traits you respect and appreciate. Include endearing qualities you adore. Record every helpful or noble thing he's done for you and your family or in service to others. Remark on physical, intellectual, and spiritual qualities. Point out *everything* good about him. Nothing is too small to mention. Take nothing for granted. After a week or two of creating your list, tuck it into a special envelope or pretty package. Tie the letter with a ribbon or to a single rose or other favorite flower. Even the masculine man will appreciate such a gift.

You could also read it to your loved one over a romantic candle-lit dinner.

"To love and to be loved is the greatest happiness of existence."
- Sydney Smith, 18th Century English Author

Afterward, consider framing your letter and putting it in a place where you can both view it often. Get creative. Make a monument out of it.

And as the days unfold, keep pen and paper handy so you can always be creating a new list. As you sit at a stop-light or wait in line at the bank or a store, be ever mindful of the blessings your mate brings to your life, and share it with him often.

9

THE LEGACY OF A LETTER

"Words that picture a special future act like a campfire on a dark night. They can draw a person toward the warmth of genuine concern and fulfilled potential. Instead of leaving a child to head into a dark unknown, they can illuminate a pathway lined with hope and purpose."
- John Trent and Gary Smalley,
The Blessing

"Family is not an important thing. It's everything."
- Michael J. Fox

W hat if you could give your children and grandchildren a gift they would cherish their entire life? And what if that gift cost little more than your time?

Not long after the death of his father, Greg Vaughn was digging through things in his garage when he came across an old tackle box. "There I was," he recalls, "standing in my dirty garage, … staring at the rusty fishing equipment inherited after the death of my father. Angry with my father. Angry with myself. Angry with God. With tears running down my face, I yelled, '*God!* Is this it? Is this all I have from the life of my father? I don't even have his signature!'"

Then, at the peak of Greg's desperation for something personal from his father to hold on to, something happened. "I heard the still, small voice of the Spirit whisper a question that pierced my soul; 'Greg, if you were to die today, what would your children hold in their hands tomorrow that would let them know they were the treasures of your life?' " He had to admit that, just like his father, he hadn't given them such a treasure.

This experience stirred Greg to search for a meaningful way to leave a legacy to his children, a way to express his love for them and his pride in them. Inspired by the ideas in the book *The Blessing*, by John Trent and Gary

"What can you do to promote world peace?
Go home and love your family." - Mother Teresa

Smalley, Greg decided to give each of his children special handwritten letters.

He bought fine stationery, leather binders and a mahogany box for each son and daughter. And then he took the idea a step further: He sought the support and camaraderie of other men, all fathers, whom he thought might be interested in bestowing a blessing on their children. He invited twelve men to lunch, and to his amazement, fourteen showed up.

One of the men suggested they first write letters to their wives, but some of the men needed persuading. They were concerned about the reactions they might receive. "What if she laughs at me?" one man said. Others worried that their wives might respond critically or with apathy.

Ultimately, they pushed through their fears and uneasiness and wrote the letters to their wives. The results were amazing. Many of the men said it was the best thing that had ever happened to their marriage.

Having received such positive feedback, the men felt encouraged to then write to their sons and daughters, and many of the reactions to those letters were just as rewarding. "I love my letters," Greg's daughter Becky said. "Daughters have this incredible longing to be blessed and

"No matter what you've done for yourself or humanity, if you can't look back on having given love and attention to your own family, what have you really accomplished?" - Lee Iacocca

loved by their father, and to read that love in a letter from my dad, it's the greatest gift a father could ever give."

Greg went on to write a life-changing book called *Letters from Dad*, that has inspired thousands of men (and women) to engage in leaving meaningful legacies to their sons and daughters in the form of handwritten letters.

It's a significant gift to receive words of love, pride, and affirmation from our parents. We get our initial sense of self-esteem and self-worth from them, especially in our formative years. It's vital to a healthy emotional and psychological make-up to receive love and validation from our mothers and fathers.

Sadly, people who don't get the affirmation they craved as children can spend adult years longing for unconditional love and approval.

Fortunately, it's never too late to give this gift to your offspring. Ellen Kreidman, Ph.D., author of the *New York Times* best-seller *Light His Fire,* emphasizes the importance of expressing unconditional love to one's mate and children. As part of her *Light His Fire* and *Light Her Fire* programs, she recommends reading *The Way Mothers Are,* a simple children's book written in 1963 by Miriam Schlein. Although the message of unconditional love is aimed at

"Your family and your love must be cultivated like a garden. Time, effort, and imagination must be summoned constantly to keep any relationship flourishing and growing." - Jim Rohn

young children, she's witnessed grown men crying upon finally receiving longed-for words of unconditional love and acceptance from parents.

Whether your children are young or grown, they want your approval and support. Handwriting a letter is a significant way to bless and affirm them.

Through such a loving gesture, you can create a solid bond and pass on a strong and lasting legacy of love.

PROMPTS

Write a letter or, preferably, many to your children, no matter their ages or situations, whether they're close or far, geographically or emotionally. And if you have stepchildren, write them, too, since they surely long for love and a blessing as well. If you don't have children, write to your niece and nephew.

Ultimately, the purpose of your letter is to lovingly validate, uplift, and encourage your children in your handwriting and

"A happy family is but an earlier heaven."
- George Bernard Shaw

with your special touch. Let them clearly know they're worthy and valuable, deeply loved and cared about. Our words of unconditional love and acceptance can be a healing balm. Tell them their life makes a significant difference.

We can help fulfill their deep need for belonging and their reason for living. Even more, our words of faith and encouragement can empower them to fulfill their highest potential and destiny. Even if your son or daughter is currently off course, your affirming, loving words can be just what he or she needs to head in the right direction again.

Recall moments of pride in them. Tell them about the gifts and talents and potential you see in them. List specific things you love, appreciate, admire, and respect.

Reminisce on paper about special moments you've shared and treasured memories. You can include inspiring family

"My father gave me the greatest gift anyone could give another person, he believed in me." - Jim Valvano

love stories or recall how various family members have triumphed over obstacles, heartache, and pain. Paint a picture of victory for your children (young or grown.) Give them a vision of a bright and beautiful future, a life full of possibilities. Do your best to focus on their dreams and hearts desires. Let them know you believe in them. Through practices like this, we can create a special bond and a sacred connection with our children.

10

THE ART OF A
KEEPSAKE LETTER

*"A letter is a blessing, a great and
all-too-rare privilege that can turn a private
moment into an exalted experience."*
- Alexandra Stoddard

"Anyone who has given love will live on in another's heart."
- Unknown

I love collecting pretty pads of paper, scented stationary, embossed envelopes, floral stickers, colored waxes and heart-or flower- shaped seals to dip in hot colored wax and seal my envelopes. There are many beautiful and creative ways to design a letter worth saving. And you can have tremendous fun in the process!

PROMPTS

Collect greeting cards with photos of hearts, flowers, romantic gardens, oceans, and scenes of nature, cute animals, or any images that appeal to you. There are countless options in gift stores, specialty shops, bookstores, and craft stores such as (Hobby Lobby and Michael's.) Choose cards that are blank on the inside so you have plenty of room to write your personal message.

Gather stylish note pads, scented stationery, pretty paper with dried flowers pressed into it, colored and fine stationery,

"Life emits a fragrance like flowers and sweet scented herbs."
- Henry David Thoreau

whatever you favor. (I love Carol's Rose Garden Stationery & Paper Products.)

Use fragrant ink as well as lively colors or other art mediums like paint, pencil, or charcoal. Try your hand at calligraphy. Practice writing cursive.

Seek and save inspirational quotes, poems, sacred scriptures, beloved verses, quotes from famous letters and favorite songs and movies. You can even include a prayer and a blessing in your letter.

Collect lovely little blank books and journals and write notes and letters in them to the people who are special to you. Tie an organza or colorful tulle ribbon around them and present them to your loved ones.

Put your letters in a special box. Use lace or ribbon in creative ways. Glue on glitter or apply pretty stickers. Paste a special photo or a piece of your artwork inside or on the cover of your card or letter.

"Starting is so beautiful."
- Rainer Rilke

Write your own ideas here as you think of them!

- ❤ _____
- ❤ _____
- ❤ _____
- ❤ _____
- ❤ _____
- ❤ _____

Have fun creating something extra special for your loved ones. Be as whimsical and playful as you like. Follow your heart and your creative impulses and enjoy the process. But you don't need to be a crafty or artistic person—just have a sincere desire to make a positive difference. Your thoughtfulness will be remembered for years, and your card or letter will be a gift that's treasured forever.

FAVORITE LETTERS

"What cannot a letter inspire? They have souls; they can speak; they have in them all that force which expresses the transports of the heart; they have the fire of our passions."
- Heloise to Abelard

"Love is our true destiny. We do not find the true meaning of life by ourselves alone-we find it with another." - Thomas Merton

While working on this book, I was thrilled to discover that so many people share my enthusiasm for the handwritten letter. I'd sent out an email to friends and family and I was often covered in goose bumps and touched to tears as many shared their handwritten letters. I wish I had room to include them all.

I'm grateful to have had the privilege and pleasure of reading your treasured notes and letters. Thank you for sharing them.

Favorite Letters

Here are a few of my favorites printed with permission. Some of the names have been changed for privacy as requested.

Love Letters

Dear Rick,

You are probably wondering why you are receiving a letter from me in the mail at your work. E-mail seemed too impersonal and there is too much to say in person. At least in a handwritten letter I have your complete attention ... I was thinking today and yesterday and the day before that I never just say "thank you."

If I had one minute left to live, I would want to be with you, sitting on a park bench, maybe by the ocean, but it really wouldn't matter where, just as long as I could tell you that I love you ... and I love the life we have.
Love,
Pepper

Hi Lover,

In the past two years, I've grown closer to you than any other man in my life. I love and appreciate so many things about you ... your loving and tender presence, the way you listen, comfort, and hold me when I'm hurting, the way you put your hand on my heart, the way you hold my hand

> *"There is nothing holier, in this life of ours, than the first consciousness of love - the first fluttering of its silken wings."*
> *- Henry Wadsworth Longfellow*

when I'm angry ... the way you understand relationships and the deeper aspects of life, and how acknowledging you are – you see my value and gifts. I love the way you affirm me – no one has ever called me beautiful and gorgeous. I feel like the luckiest girl for All the ways you love and appreciate me.

I just wanted to acknowledge and celebrate all the good that you've given me over the past two years ... and all that you continue to give. I appreciate you in my life. That's what an anniversary means to me.

I love you with all my heart, Jenny

∽

Dear Jenny,

You have so much courage my love! So much courage in all that you have faced to grow into who you are today ... a radiant, open-hearted woman who makes others feel accepted, like they belong and have value. Through all that you've been through, you are still unjaded and are a living, breathing reminder of aliveness, joy and innocence.

I am so proud to watch you move forward in becoming even more useful and deliberate in the application of the gift of presence you have so abundantly. I have no doubt that you will land in your right livelihood that feels empowering, fulfilling, joyful, and as natural to you as breathing. You have everything you need to embody this. I see you and I love you. Thank you for being in my life.

Love,

Rob

Dear Lover,

Today we celebrate three years of love shared. My heart is overflowing with love for you. Isn't this a cute card! Hummingbirds' symbolize lightness of being and enjoying the sweetness of life. We are in such a light and sweet place in our relationship right now. I can't even find the words to express how deeply grateful I am that we have made

"A joyful heart is the inevitable result of a heart burning with love." - Mother Teresa

_____

it here …. You becoming more of who you really are, is the most precious gift I have been given on my 40th birthday … and ever! I'm so grateful God has given me such a vulnerable, real, deep, sexy, passionate, smart man.

I cherish you, baby. Looking forward to many more years in your arms. Giving you all my love.
Jenny

———

Babe,

It [Valentine's Day] is a special day in our life. The day you said yes! Forever changed <u>me and us.</u> Although we are apart, we are always together in each others heart.
Love! <u>Me</u>!

"Friends confirm us."
- Alexandra Stoddard

~⌒~

My Love,

If there were an Olympic event for the world's best husband, you would win the gold for sure!
Your Mrs.

Friendship

~⌒~

Dearest D,

You are amazing. I love what you've done with your home. I love what you've done with your life and your family. I <u>love</u> being here … immersed in beauty … immersed in your presence and the love of your family. I love that you love being a mother and are so conscious of creating unity and love and possibilities for your family.

Thank you for so generously sharing your home with us and giving us such a glorious glimpse into abundance. I feel such a sense

> *"Love in action can only produce happiness."*
> *- Don Miguel Ruiz*

of expansion and bounty at your place, a tremendous scope for possibility and dreams coming true … I can feel God here. Your home is healing and happy and good for me. I am relaxed to the core of my being. Thank you …

Victoria

Dear M,

How sweet and soothing and healing your words are to me. I've heard it said that my best friends are the ones who bring out the best in me. I would also add; who believe the best about me, who see me as I am and love me (strengths and flaws). I always feel better, affirmed, validated, valuable, and loved when I talk to you. I am truly thankful for you and your love and how you handle me and our friendship so kindly and reverently. What a true treasure our friendship is.

Victoria

"No act of kindness is ever wasted."
- Aesop

Family

Spencer,

St. Christopher is regarded as the "Patron Saint of Travelers." This is one that I have worn for years and he has watched over me and I know he will do the same for you. After you wear it for awhile, there will come a time you won't even notice you have it on, but when you do notice, think of me and know I'm thinking of you.

Love,

Dad

From a twenty-year-old to his stepmother:

Happy Mother's Day!

I really am lucky to have you in my life. You have been there for me since day one and have truly blessed my life.

Love,

Josh

"To do more for the world than the world does for you, that is success." - Henry Ford

~⌐

From a seventeen-year-old to his mother on her fifty-first birthday.

> *Mom's 51st*
>
> 1. *You are the most selfless person I have ever known*
> 2. *You are the best mom anyone could ever ask for*
> 3. *You are always going out of your way to do things for me*
> 4. *You never complain about our relationship*
> 5. *For being 51 you still are absolutely beautiful (even when you wear the same jeans)*
> 6. *We think so much alike it's not even funny*
> 7. *You see my ambitions when I loose sight*
> 8. *You always seem to be in a good mood even when you're not*
> 9. *You have a great personality and you always hold your head up high*

"Praise is one of the strongest forms of love," - Catherine Ponder, The Prospering Power of Love

10. *You are the hardest working person I know, always trying to improve my life for the future.*

I love you mommy!
    I hope and pray you have a blessed year to come!
Your son,
Joshua Michael Rossi
p.s. if anything is misspelled I get that from you :)

⸻

From a mother to her son on his fortieth birthday:
    Hope you're still celebrating … This is a little late, but Dad and I remember your birth all the time, so we celebrate the day as if it were today. We were excited to have a blondie, cute as can be! And he developed into a handsome, intelligent, sweet, wonderful, funny, giving, loving, silly, strong, generous, kind, supportive, gentle spirit … That's our son … We love you! Mom and Dad

_____

‿つ

This letter is from an eighty-three-year-old Dutch native to her sister, Monique, an eighty-four-year-old nun in Denver. They travel to see each other three times a year and hand write letters in between their visits.

Sr. Monigue,

Each person carries its own backpack through life. In it he carries everything that was weighing heavily as well as his air bubbles. We prefer to stuff as many beautiful moments as possible in our back packs, but during our hike we also walk through weather and wind. Sometimes it becomes slightly damaged. We continue to walk firmly and arrive naturally at an open place in the forest in which the sun is shining on us again. That's where naturally emerges a golden glow on our backpack.

Tine

"The best thing to hold onto in life is each other."
- Audrey Hepburn"

⌁

Sr. Monigue,

Twenty-five years of love and sorrow your backpack was heavy but together we made it lighter. Since we became pilgrims it became even lighter. We filled our backpacks with beautiful experiences, special encounters, joy and especially gratitude. Let us stay in wonder and hopefully we may continue to enjoy what is on our path for a long time.

Tine, your twin soul

⌁

I fondly remember when my friend from work clutched a letter to her chest as she told me about it. It was from her eighty-year-old aunt, whom she'd always cherished and adored. "If I could be like anyone in the world, it would be her," she said, beaming as she clung to the letter. "And look, there's something about her handwriting that's different than the way people write today." I agreed—her aunt's penmanship reminded me of my own grandmother's letters.

"Love cures people, both the ones who give it and the ones who recieve it." - *Karl Menninger*

Also among the stories that touched my heart was a note written on the back of a framed "World's Greatest Mother" certificate given to Melba by her daughter Toni, her senior year of college. Toni found this note a few weeks after her mother died at eighty-three.

"I don't know if I was the World's Greatest Mother, but I loved you with all of my strength."

Words are powerful. And we are forever touched by their eternal nature. Use your words for good. Use them to uplift, empower, and encourage people. Spread love, joy, and goodness in the world with a handwritten note or letter.

ACKNOWLEDGMENTS

*"Let us be grateful to the people that
make us happy: they are the charming
gardeners who make our souls blossom."*
- Marcel Proust

"Blessed is the influence of a true, loving human soul on another." - George Eliot

---

It would take an entire book to include all the people who have contributed, influenced, inspired, and supported me in one way or another, in person or in spirit, in the writing of this book. To each of you I owe great gratitude, and I thank you, from the deepest place in my heart.

The first person I want to thank is Dawn Michelle Cassaday, who enthusiastically urged me to write this book.

I also drew inspiration from authors whose wisdom, encouragement, and excellent instruction helped me move this book forward: Andrea Costantine and Lisa Shultz, *How to Bring Your Book to Life This Year: An Exploratory Guidebook on Writing and Self-Publishing*; Dan Poynter, *Writing Nonfiction: Turning Thoughts Into Books*; Chip Richards, *Writing the Story Within*; Sanaya Roman, *Becoming a Writer*; Joel Osteen, *You Can, You Will*; Victoria Osteen, *Love Your Life*; Lucille Zimmerman, *Renewed: Finding Your Inner Happy in an Overwhelmed World*; Janice Campbell, *Choosing Your Bigger Yes: Five Steps to an Authentically Happy Life*; and Alexandra Stoddard, *Gift of a Letter*.

A special thank-you to Toni Robino and Doug Wagner of Windword Literary Services for their BookWalk

"Only a life lived for others is a life worthwhile."
- Albert Einstein

coaching program and editorial services. I'm especially grateful for their wonderful ideas and wise suggestions while still honoring my voice. They both were gracious, professional, and beyond helpful and made the whole experience easier and more enjoyable.

I am grateful to Polly Letofsky of My Word Publishing, my publishing consultant and book project manager, for her encouragement, enthusiasm, and excellent advice as well as for helping me handle all the hairy details of publishing my book and making it widely available. Plus, her fun-loving, lighthearted spirit made her an absolute joy to work with.

Another special thank-you to Nick Zelinger my book cover and logo designer. He is way talented, creative, understanding, easy to talk to and overall fantastic to work with.

My deep gratitude to Andrea Costantine, the interior designer of my book. I loved her creative ideas and style. She always seemed to know exactly what I wanted, which made the book layout process exciting and fun! Even more, Andrea has a calming presence. She was very patient with me and such a pleasure to work with.

As for the bright, beautiful women in my Heart

"Being deeply loved by someone gives you strength, while loving someone deeply gives you courage." - Lao Tzu

Storming Group, first and foremost I want to thank my sweet friend Jenny Domingue, who invited me to the group and who has believed in me and supported me through it all. And to Kathryn Severns Avery for calling me at that pivotal point when I asked God for a sign, thank you for being a divine instrument and for your guidance and encouragement. And a heartfelt thank-you to all the other remarkable women in the group: Maryann Brown, Susanne Hoogwater, Christy Wessler, Anita Larson, Jena Sawyer, Sally Evans, and Tina Blakely.

A huge, wholehearted thank you to my family and dear friends; Gloria Vigil, Orlando Vigil, Orley Vigil, Michelle Vigil, Jordan Vigil, Tanner Vigil, Talley Vigil, Bill Bishop, Dianne Faust, James Bishop Faust, Robert H. Russell II, Catharyn Baird, Jerry Gray, Doreen Rossi, Roxy Falsetto, Tonya Williams, Ann Sheflin, Christy Richards, Trish Elledge, Gina Alianiello, and Kiddo.

And to my precious mother, the first person to encourage me to follow my heart and be a writer. She made her transition to heaven before the publication of this book but I know she is with me in spirit. Mom, I love and miss you more than words can say. Thank you for all your love and support.

"Love is an action, a power of the soul."

- Erich Fromm

And finally, to my beloved husband Aaron, the love of my life and healing balm to my soul. Thank you for your unending love and devotion. You are the kindest, most giving and unselfish person I have ever known. Your love causes me to bubble over with joy and write notes and letters.

ABOUT THE AUTHOR

Ronna Vigil has a passion for helping people to create strong, fulfilling relationships and heart-to-heart connections, especially with handwritten notes and letters. She credits this practice for blessing her life and her relationships with extraordinary love and happiness. Her education in holistic health & well-being and interpersonal communication as well as her personal experience and the results she's seen in others has affirmed to her that the written word has magical healing powers. Ronna lives near the foothills of the beautiful Colorado Rocky Mountains with her husband, Aaron, and their pooch, Lily. You can connect with her on her website at www.ronnavigil.com